Golden Foot

Golden Foot

A Jataka Tale

Inspired by Nazli Gellek
Adapted by Karen Stone
Illustrated by Rosalyn White

Dharma Publishing

Jataka Tales Series

Cover design by Kando Dorsey, endpapers by Margie Horton
Third edition 2009, revised and augmented with
guidance for parents and teachers.

Printed on acid-free paper.

Printed in the United States of America by Dharma Press
35788 Hauser Bridge Road, Cazadero, California 95421

9   8   7   6   5   4   3   2   1

Library of Congress Control Number: 2009938991
ISBN 978-089800-517-2

Dedicated to children everywhere

Once upon a time, a royal stag lived in a forest in ancient India. He was a creature of grace and beauty, with a coat the color of gold. His horns rose above his head like a silver wreath, and his eyes shone like round jewels. So brightly did his hooves sparkle in the sunlight that his friends called him Golden Foot.

Hundreds of deer honored the great stag as their king. From among them, Golden Foot chose Graceful, a young doe, to be his queen. Living peacefully together in the great pine forest, they had no fear of danger.

Early one morning, before the sun had risen, a hunter
came to the forest to lay a trap. With a rope he made a
noose that he hid among the pines along a grassy path.
At the end of the path was a cool, fresh spring where
the deer came to drink when they were thirsty.

That day, Golden Foot came down the path alone, with Graceful and the other deer following behind him. As he approached the stream he caught his foot in the hidden snare.

Golden Foot pulled this way and that but could not free himself. The more he struggled, the tighter the noose became, until he cried out in pain. Hearing his cries, the entire herd panicked and fled.

Graceful searched for her mate amongst the many deer. When she did not find him, she ran back along the grassy path to the stream. There was Golden Foot, weary and sad. Graceful said, "Golden Foot, you are stronger than you think. Try to use all your strength to break your bonds!"

Yet, try as he might, Golden Foot could not free himself. Seeing that his struggle seemed hopeless, Graceful thought, "None of the deer in our herd will survive without their leader to guide them."

She comforted him saying, "Don't be afraid, Golden Foot. I shall stay close by. When your captor comes I shall plead for your freedom."

It was not long before they heard the hunter crashing through the brush. When he stood before them, he carried a huge sword in one hand and a sharp-pointed knife in the other. His eyes revealed his cruel intent. Slowly, Graceful went forward to meet him.

Remaining at a respectful distance, Graceful greeted the hunter and said, "You have captured my mate, the stag Golden Foot, wise beyond compare. Please, spare the life of the king of deer, and take my life instead."

Hearing her speak, the hunter was dumbfounded. "Even human beings do not give up their lives for their king, or for their mates. What are these creatures?"

The hunter's heart was moved and, gazing at the doe, he thought, "This exquisite creature speaks to me in the language of men! She has won my heart. Today, I will grant life to her and to her mate, the magnificent stag." In the spirit of kindness, he set Golden Foot free.

Golden Foot, the king of the deer, thought, "This hunter has spared us and saved all my friends who would otherwise have lost their leader. We must offer him a precious gift in return."

Going to the roots of a tree nearby, he struck the ground with his pointed hoof and unearthed three shining, magic jewels.

Golden Foot offered the jewels to the hunter and said, "My friend, with these wish-fulfilling gems, you and your family will be protected. You will never again need to take the life of another creature. Wherever you go, offer your help to those in need."

Reminding the hunter to heed these words, the stag and the doe disappeared into the forest, where they lived in peace and harmony to the end of their days.

The Jataka Tales nurture in readers young and old an appreciation for values shared by all the world's great traditions. Read aloud, performed and studied for centuries, they communicate universal values such as kindness, forgiveness, compassion, humility, courage, honesty and patience. You can bring these stories alive through the suggestions on these pages. Actively engaging with the stories creates a bridge to the children in your life and opens a dialogue about what brings joy, stability and caring.

Golden Foot

A doe named Graceful offers her life to save her mate, Golden Foot, the king of the deer, who is entangled in a hunter's snare. The hunter is so impressed with Graceful's offer that he frees the royal stag. In return, Golden Foot offers the hunter three wish-fulfilling jewels that will protect the hunter's family. The hunter promises never to take the life of another being and to offer help to those in need.

Key Values
Love
Sacrificing for
a noble cause
Helping others

Bringing the story to life

Engage the children by saying, "This story takes place in a deep forest in India where a royal stag lives with his mate and herd. One day a clever hunter captures Golden Foot with a snare. What do you think happens next? Let's read the story to find out."

- Why is the stag named Golden Foot? Why is he followed by the other deer?
- How does the hunter trap Golden Foot, and what do the other deer do?
- What offer does Golden Foot's mate Graceful make to the hunter? How does he respond? Can you imagine anyone making such an offer?
- What would happen if the deer herd lost their king, Golden Foot?
- What does Golden Foot give to the hunter? Why?
- How is the hunter changed at the end of the story?

Discussion topics and questions can be modified depending on the child's age.

Teaching values through play

Follow up on the storytelling with creative activities that explore the characters and values and appeal to the five senses.

Have the children construct and decorate character masks for the hunter, Golden Foot, and his mate. Act out the story, and then have the children switch roles. Ask: "How does it feel to be the hunter? The one who is hunted?"

- The children follow the lead deer who pours them their favorite drink; they can then sit and drink in a comfortable spot in the house or school.
- With the other children in another room, have the hunter set out a snare (such as a piece of paper with a drawing on it) and then hide as the deer follow Golden Foot to a place of treats. What happens when he comes across the trap? Have a discussion about what it feels like when a familiar place of comfort is no longer safe. Also discuss how and why the leader goes first.
- Take turns playing being a leader or parent who must bring young ones safely to a special place. What must the leader consider?

Active reading

- Before children can read, they enjoy storytelling and love growing familiar with the characters and drawings. You can show them the pictures and tell the story in your own words with characteristic voices for Graceful, Golden Foot, and the hunter.
- By reading the book to them two or three times and helping them recognize words, you help young listeners build a vocabulary.
- Carry a book whenever you leave the house in case there is some extra time for reading.
- Display the key values on the refrigerator or a bulletin board – at child's eye level – and refer to them in your daily interactions.
- Use the story's wisdom when something is upsetting. When one child takes another's toys or food, or says something mean, ask, "What would Graceful do?" Or "Remember how the hunter changed? Why did that happen?"

- Ask the children about a time when someone sacrificed something to help them (perhaps a parent did not sleep to take care of a sick child). See if the children can remember times of such caring.

Daily activities

Integrate the wisdom of this story into daily life. Have discussions over dinner or while working around the house: "What makes a good leader? Who is willing to sacrifice for another?"

When you and the children visit the zoo or if you have a pet, notice the habits of animals and how they tend to behave in the same ways (how and what they eat, where they sleep, etcetera). Think about how a hunter can trap them. Also think about how knowing those habits can help someone to protect and care for them.

Encourage the children to look for opportunities to help another person doing a hard task (carrying in and putting away all the groceries; taking out the garbage; cleaning up). The children don't have to be like Graceful and offer up their lives, but what happens if they help the "leader" a little bit?

We are grateful for the opportunity to offer these Jataka Tales to you. May they inspire fresh insight into the dynamics of human relationships and may understanding grow with each reading.

These adaptations of Jataka Tales are for children aged three to eight

JATAKA TALES SERIES